WILDFLOWERS
AROUND
THE
WORLD

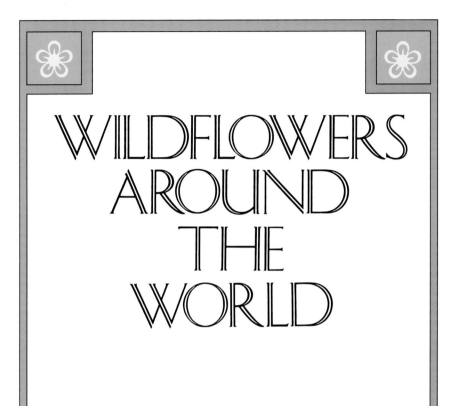

WILDFLOWERS AROUND THE WORLD

BY ELAINE LANDAU

A FIRST BOOK
FRANKLIN WATTS
NEW YORK/LONDON/TORONTO/SYDNEY/1991

Cover photograph courtesy of: Bob Clemenz Landscape Photography

Photographs courtesy of: Bill Ratcliffe: pp. 2, 42, 44;
Animals Animals/Earth Scenes: pp. 12 (Michael P. Gadomski),
15 (Ted Levin), 16, 30 (both Jack Wilburn), 24 (Tom Edwards),
26 (Richard Kolar), 28, 33, 34 (all John Gerlach), 41 (B. G. Murray,
Jr.), 46 (Karen Tweedy-Holmes); E. R. Degginger: pp. 20,
50; Horticultural Society of New York: pp. 23, 52; New York
Botanical Garden: p. 38; New York Public Library, Picture
Collection: p. 49.

Library of Congress Cataloging-in-Publication Data

Landau, Elaine.
Wildflowers around the world / by Elaine Landau.
p.   cm.—(A First book)
Includes bibliographical references (p.   ) and index.
Summary: Describes the types of flowers that grow in various
climates and environments around the world.
ISBN 0-531-20005-1
1. Wild Flowers—Juvenile literature.   [1. Wild flowers.]
I. Title. II. Series.
QK85.5.L36 1991
582.13—dc20   90-13090 CIP

CONTENTS

For Iris—
both a lovely flower and a wonderful person

INTRODUCTION

Wildflowers add color and beauty to natural landscapes throughout the world. Numerous types of flowers exist in all sorts of environments. Wildflowers grow naturally in mountain meadows, swamps, jungles, along seacoasts, on prairies, and deserts, as well as in countless other areas.

For thousands of years, people have enjoyed wildflowers. Colorful wildflowers have been worn on special occasions, used to decorate homes, and used as an ingredient in the manufacture of various perfumes. In many cultures, flowers have their place at various social functions. Often they may be found at both weddings and funerals.

Although wildflowers are not considered a major food source, some flower petals are edible. Wildflowers have also been used to make wines and brandies. Honey, a natural sweetener, comes from flowers as well.

Once wildflowers were the only blossoms in existence. However, in time, people found they could grow their own flowers by planting seeds. They learned to develop special types of flowers in *greenhouses* and gardens.

Yet flowers growing naturally in the wild are still abundant. This book is about those blossoms that spring up on their own to enhance our environment.

(Note: the scientific name of the flower is in brackets and italicized, following the common name.)

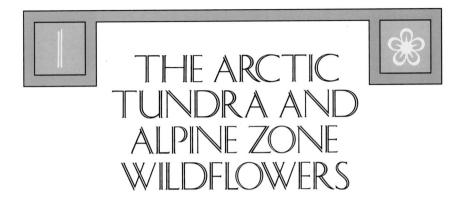

THE ARCTIC TUNDRA AND ALPINE ZONE WILDFLOWERS

The Arctic tundra is a distant northern region that extends across three continents—Asia, Europe, and North America. The Arctic tundra tends to be cold, dry, and somewhat barren. Grasses and mosses largely cover this area. There are some dwarf trees, but the climate is too inhospitable for them to grow tall.

There isn't a very long growing season in the Arctic tundra. The freezing temperatures tend to keep the ground frozen. However, during the spring and summer months, the soil's surface finally begins to thaw. During this brief period, a variety of blossoms spring up.

Alpine zones lie high in mountainous regions. In some ways, conditions in Alpine zones are very much like those of the Arctic tundra. Both areas tend to be somewhat cold and do not receive a great deal of rainfall or moisture.

11

Labrador Tea

Yet a number of attractive wildflowers thrive in the Alpine zones of the world. These flowers tend to grow well in rocky environments. Alpine zones are found in North America's Rocky Mountains, Europe's Alps, and the Himalaya mountain range of Asia as well as in other areas, such as the Andes in South America and the New Zealand Alps.

LABRADOR TEA
Scientific name: [*Ledum groenlandicum*]

The small white flowers of the Labrador tea have five petals and grow in umbrella-like clusters. Labrador tea is common in the alpine Sierra Nevada mountains of eastern California, as well as in other areas in northern and subarctic North America. The flowers may also be found in Greenland and parts of northern Europe. Regardless of where they grow, these beautiful blossoms thrive best in moist, boggy spots.

The Labrador tea's leaves are oblong and fragrant. Over the years, individuals have found the plant's leaves useful in a number of ways. The leaves have a mild *narcotic* effect when brewed, and have sometimes been used in producing beer as well as a *medicinal* tea. In addition, the plant leaves also yield a substance known as tannin. Tannin has been used to treat animal hides so they may be fashioned into leather goods.

Labrador tea is a member of the Heath plant family. The Heath family largely consists of low evergreen plants from which flowers often bloom. Depending on the plant, these flowers may be white or a variety of bright colors.

SKY PILOT
Scientific name: [*Polemonium viscosum*]

Sky pilots have purple, funnel-shaped flowers and numerous tiny round *leaflets*. They are found in both arctic and alpine environments at heights of 9,000 to 12,000 feet (2,700 to 3,600 m). These flowers are called sky pilots because they grow in such high regions. They bloom between June and August.

Sky pilots are commonly found in the Rocky Mountains from the southwestern United States north to Alberta, Canada, as well as in other areas. They sometimes sprout up between cracks in rocky regions.

Sky pilots are colorful and attractive to look at, but have a foul odor. These flowers also give off a sticky substance that has been known to stick to hikers' shoes.

The colorful sky pilot is a member of the Phlox flower family. This grouping contains about 300 different *species* or types of flowers. Most of the flowers within this family have five petals that join together at the flower's base.

Sky Pilot

Wild Heliotrope

WILD HELIOTROPE
Scientific name: [*Phacelia sericea*]

Wild heliotrope grows from 4 to 18 inches (10 to 46 cm) high and bears clusters of open, bell-shaped flowers. These blossoms are usually bluish-purple in color, although some may be white. The flowers bloom in dense clusters on the upper portion of the stems.

The wild heliotrope's leaves are usually between 1 and 5 inches (2.5 to 13 cm) long. The leaves feel silky when touched and are covered with silvery hairs.

These flowers usually bloom in June and July. They are commonly found at high altitudes on the rocky slopes of mountainous regions. They have also frequently been spotted bordering mountain forests.

The flower's scientific name comes from two Greek words. The Greek word *phakelos* means "bunch" or "group." The plant's blossoms tend to grow in thick bunches at its stem's top. The Greek word *sericia* means "silky," and describes the soft downy leaves. Sometimes these flowers are also called purple fringe because of their color.

Wild heliotrope is a member of the Waterleaf family. Both American Indians and early American settlers used some of the plants in this family for food.

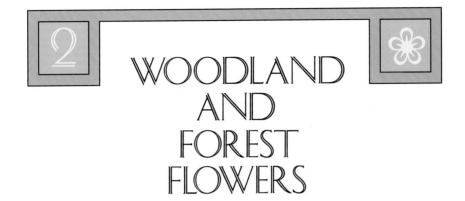

WOODLAND AND FOREST FLOWERS

Many types of flowers bloom in wooded areas outside of the tropics. (For tropical wildflowers, see chapter 5.) Coniferous forests (the majority of the trees have long slender leaves shaped like needles and are evergreen) may be found throughout much of Canada and the northern sections of both Europe and Asia. Coniferous forests also often exist at the lower levels of the Rocky Mountains and in the northwestern United States.

Broadleaf forests (the majority of the trees have wide flat leaves which they lose in the fall) are especially common in the eastern United States. There are also broadleaf forests in parts of central and eastern Europe and in eastern Asia.

The growth and survival of forest flowers greatly depends on the trees surrounding them. This is because the trees largely determine how much sunlight or shade flowers growing on the forest floor will receive. Frequently, forest flowers sprout up in

Indian Pipes

the early spring. At that time of year, the trees are not as fully leafed as they will be in the summer. Therefore, the scant leaves allow the sunlight to fall directly on the flowers. When the forests become heavily shaded, flowers have less opportunity to grow since most of the sun's rays are blocked. Then wildflowers tend to crop up in clearings or around the forest borders.

INDIAN PIPES
Scientific name: [*Monotropa uniflora*]

Indian pipes are unusual bell-shaped flowers that have four to five petals. Looking like clay pipes, they rise up from the brown forest floor debris. These flowers sometimes seem to nod in the breeze.

Indian pipes are usually completely colorless. Because of this, these flowers have been called ghost flowers and corpse flowers. However, in rare instances, they take on a faint pink hue. These single flowers have thick scaly stems that are generally between 3 and 4 inches (7 to 10 cm) high. Indian pipes do not have leaves.

Indian pipes are frequently found in shady areas of coniferous forests. They are most common in the woodlands of North America and eastern Asia. Spotted among the forest's shadows, Indian pipes have been described as hauntingly beautiful.

Indian pipes lack *chlorophyll.* Chlorophyll is the substance that gives plants their green color. Plants need chlorophyll to produce food to nourish themselves. Indian pipes cannot manufacture their own food. Instead, they live off decaying matter in the forest's soil.

If an Indian pipe is picked, it will quickly turn black. In the past, American Indians used Indian pipes to make eye lotion. The flowers were thought to have healing properties.

The Indian pipe is a member of the wintergreen family.

MARSH MARIGOLD (COWSLIP)
Scientific name: [*Caltha palustris*]

Marsh marigolds are brilliant golden-yellow flowers that are rich in *nectar*. These blossoms have thick hollow stems. The marsh marigold's glossy deep green leaves are shaped somewhat like kidney beans. In some regions, these plant leaves are boiled and eaten as a vegetable.

Marsh marigolds often crop up near brooks and streams that run through wooded areas. As its name suggests, the marsh-dwelling flower thrives in damp or wet areas. American Indians called it *Onondaga*, which means "it blooms in swamps."

In spite of its name, the marsh marigold is actually not a marigold. This cup-shaped yellow blossom is a member of the buttercup family. This family is made up of about 800 different flowers.

Marsh marigolds bloom between April and June. During this time, they provide a flash of bright spring color in drab, moist, wooded areas.

Marsh Marigold

White Trillium

WHITE TRILLIUM
Scientific name: [*Trillium grandiflorum*]

The handsome white trillium, which grows singly on its stalk, bears flowers 2 to 3 inches (5 to 7.5 cm) wide. The name trillium comes from the Latin *tri* which means "three." This flower has three petals and its leaves grow in threes. White trillium, which may be found in rich wooded areas, blooms between April and June. As the flower ages, it may take on a pinkish hue.

The plant sprouts from an underground stem. Years ago, Indians used the plant's stem to cure illnesses. Someone bitten by a snake would chew on its root. It was also given to pregnant women in labor to ease childbirth.

These flowers are often considered among the most attractive early spring blossoms. Unfortunately, in many areas, they may be overpicked. As a result, white trillium has become an endangered flower.

Although white trillium does not have the word lily in its name, it is nevertheless a member of the Lily family. This means that it's related to such flowers as the desert lily (page 40) and the lily of the valley. Most lilies have white or bright flowers that extend from upright stems.

Wild Geranium

WILD GERANIUM
Scientific name: [*Geranium maculatum*]

Wild geraniums, which grow between 1 and 2 feet (30 to 60 cm) tall, bear beautiful purple flowers. The blossoms have five rounded petals and measure about an inch and a half (4 cm) across. A small, hairlike patch extends from each petal's base. Often the flowers grow in clusters of two to five blossoms. Wild geraniums usually bloom between May and June.

The plant's stem tends to be hairy, and its grayish green leaves are also covered with rough hair. Years ago, American Indians cooked the plant's young leaves and ate them as a vegetable. The leaves were also sometimes used to brew tea.

Wild geraniums are frequently found in densely wooded regions as well as in thickets and other areas. They are members of the Geranium flower family. This flower group is known for its large colorful blossoms.

Five Spot

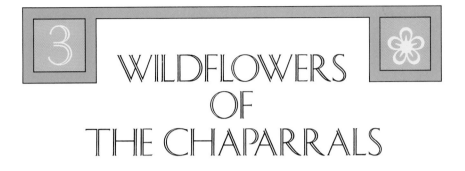

WILDFLOWERS
OF
THE CHAPARRALS

Chaparrals are areas characterized by abundantly growing shrubs and small shrublike trees. These areas are located largely in southern California, Australia, Chile, and South Africa. Chaparrals also border areas around the Mediterranean Sea.

These regions tend to enjoy warm springlike weather much of the year. The chaparrals also do not receive an overabundance of rain in the summer. Seeds tend to do well in this environment. As a result, a rich variety of colorful wildflowers grow in the chaparrals that would never survive in cooler, damper locations.

FIVE-SPOT
Scientific name: [*Nemophila maculata*]

This bell-shaped flower of the five-spot has five white petals. It gets its name from the fact that each petal has a purple marking on it.

Fiddle-neck

This flower's stem curves delicately, enhancing its graceful appearance. The five-spot has oblong leaves that divide into five to nine lobes. It blooms from April through August, and is sometimes called the calico flower. This name also reflects the flower's unusual markings.

The five-spot is a member of the Waterleaf family.

FIDDLE-NECK
Scientific name: [*Amsinckia intermedia*]

Fiddle-necks are small five-lobed, funnel-shaped flowers. They range in color from yellow to orange. The outside of the flower is covered with a thin layer of hair.

These delicate blossoms grow from a curved flower spike. In fact, the name fiddle-neck refers to the plant's unusual shape. Fiddle-necks have lance-shaped leaves between 4 and 8 inches (10 to 20 cm) long.

Fiddle-necks bloom between March and June. These flowers are common in the chaparrals of California. In some areas they are so plentiful that they seem to form a broad blanket of bright color.

The abundant flowers are an important food source for grazing livestock. The animals fatten themselves as they feed on these flowers in the fields. That's why fiddle-necks are sometimes called *Saccato Gordo,* which means "fat grass."

The fiddle-neck is a member of the Borage family. This group consists of nearly 2,000 different types of flowers. Most of these species have petals that are fused together to form a funnel-shaped blossom.

CHINESE HOUSES
Scientific name: [*Collinsia heterophylla*]

Chinese houses are lavender-blue, five-lobed flowers. Each beautiful bell-shaped blossom is divided into two lips. They grow in clusters along the plant's stem. Chinese houses have smooth lance-shaped leaves.

Chinese houses usually bloom between April and June. The gaily colored flowers are most frequently found bordering *thickets* in the chaparrals. They are especially common in California.

The flowers are called Chinese houses because their blossom clusters look somewhat like Oriental pagodas. A pagoda is a tower made of several stories, each of which has an upward curved roof. The flower's scientific name honors an eighteenth-century *botanist* named Zaccheus Collins.

Chinese houses are in the Figwort family. There are about 3,000 different types of flowers within this grouping. Most are bell shaped with thin stems. Frequently, pairs of leaves grow along the stems.

Chinese Houses

Long-beaked Stork's Bill

LONG-BEAKED STORK'S BILL
Scientific name: [*Erodium botrys*]

Long-beaked stork's bills are attractive purple flowers. They have five petals that usually grow to about a half inch (1 cm) in length. Often these flowers are found in clusters on short stalks. They bloom from April to October.

These flowers were originally found in warm regions near the Mediterranean Sea. However, the blossoms were later brought to the United States. Before long, these brilliant purple flowers could be spotted throughout portions of America's western countryside. The long-beaked stork's bill has since become a popular wildflower in southern California and other areas.

In some ways, the long-beaked stork's bill has proven to be as useful as it is pleasing to look at. Since these flowers bloom in both early spring and fall, horses and cows often graze on the wild blossoms.

The long-beaked stork's bill is a member of the Geranium family. There are about 750 different types of flowers within that grouping. Most of these flowers have five petals.

DESERT WILDFLOWERS

The deserts of the world are hot, very dry regions in which moisture is scarce. Some deserts receive less than a dozen inches (30 cm) of rain throughout an entire year. When it rains, there may be heavy downpours with lengthy droughts in between.

Desert wildflowers have adapted to these *arid* conditions. Some desert wildflowers have thick stems that hold water for the plant to use during dry spells. Often desert plants also have long roots and a waxlike coating that helps to retain water.

Many desert flowers have a very short life cycle. The seeds grow following a heavy rainstorm, producing a flower that lives only for a short period of time. Although there are desert regions in many areas of the world, the flowers described here are found in the deserts of North America.

Beavertail Cactus

BEAVERTAIL CACTUS
Scientific name: [*Opuntia basilaris*]

The beavertail cactus plant bears clusters of flowers on the upper portion of its rounded pads. These rosy red blossoms are small and cup-shaped. The flowers usually bloom between May and June.

The beavertail cactus doesn't have spines (thornlike bristles). Instead, the plant has tufts of minute bristles. These tufts may either be round or oval. The spines or stiff hairs on a cactus protect the plant from being eaten by animals. Beavertail cacti are especially common in desert areas from Utah west to California. The plant is called beavertail because the pads from which the flowers sprout look like the animal's tail.

The beavertail cactus is a member of the Cactus family. There are nearly 2,000 different types of cactus plants. All are able to survive in hot, dry areas. These plants' stems hold water, and their waxy skin helps to keep moisture from escaping.

Like the beavertail, all cactus plants sprout flowers. Some cactus flowers are white; others may be red, yellow, or orange. Cactus flowers do not last very long. Some bloom for several days, but others may not even last a full day. After a cactus flower blooms, it dries up and falls from the plant. Even though its flowers may not last very long, cactuses tend to be hardy. Some botanists believe these plants have existed on earth for millions of years.

DESERT LILY
Scientific name: [*Hesperocallis undulata*]

These large white trumpet-shaped flowers of the desert lily spread open into splendid blossoms. Greenish streaks of color appear on the backs of the six sections of each flower. These flowers are commonly found in the Mojave Desert, the Colorado desert, western Arizona, and in other areas. Desert lilies bloom between March and May. At one time, American Indians ate these large blossoms.

The desert lily is a member of the lily family, one of the largest flower families. These flowers usually grow from scaly bulbs and do best in deep sandy soil that is rich in clay.

There are about 4,000 different types of lilies, among which is the well-known lily of the valley.

Desert Lily

Wild Four O'Clock

WILD FOUR O'CLOCK
Scientific name: [*Mirabilis multiflora*]

The four o'clock, which grows to about 18 inches (46 cm) in height, bears colorful red-purple blossoms. Its flower is funnel-shaped and generally tends to be about 2 inches (5 cm) long.

The brilliant blossoms seem to spring out from their long stalks. The flower is called the four o'clock because its blossoms tend to open late in the day, toward evening. Wild four o'clocks usually bloom between April and September.

The plant has broad oval leaves covered with a fine layer of hair. A portion of the plant's Latin name refers to its appearance. The word *mirabilis* means "marvelous." At times, American Indians used the wild four o'clock's root as a medicine. They believed it could relieve some types of stomach pains.

The wild four o'clock is a member of the Four o'clock family. Most of the flowers in this family do not have petals. Instead, they tend to be funnel-shaped. There are about 290 different flowers in this grouping.

Sand Blazing Star

SAND BLAZING STAR
Scientific name: [*Mentzelia involucrata*]

The sand blazing star is a plant that has large yellowish white flowers. At times, these beautiful five-petaled blossoms look almost as if they were made of satin.

The plant on which the flower blooms is usually about 16 inches (41 cm) tall and has barbed prickly hairs. Its grayish green heart-shaped leaves have tiny spines.

Sand blazing stars may be found in the Mojave and Colorado deserts as well as in other desert areas of the southwestern United States. As with any plant found in these regions, the sand blazing star is able to survive strong winds, low rainfall, and severe extremes of both heat and cold. Following a favorable spring rainfall, these dazzling wildflowers beautify the dusty landscape.

The sand blazing star is a member of the Stickleaf family. There are about 250 different types of flowers within that grouping. Most of these may be found growing in North America.

Gloxinia

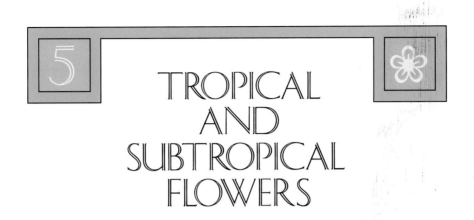

TROPICAL AND SUBTROPICAL FLOWERS

The steamy warm weather conditions of tropical and subtropical regions help to produce a stunning array of magnificent wildflowers. Thousands of varieties of flowers bloom in the tropical rain forests of South and Central America. Hawaii too is known for its rich assortment of colorful flowers.

Large numbers of subtropical flowers are found in South Africa and the southernmost portion of China. Within the continental United States, lovely subtropical flowers grow in the lower portion of Florida.

GLOXINIA
Scientific name: [*Sinningia speciosa*]

The gloxinia's trumpet-shaped blossoms may be either purple, white, or deep red. At times, these flowers may be streaked or spotted with darker hues. The plant's green leaves look and feel like velvet. Gloxinias grow wild in the tropics of Brazil. They are also frequently cultivated in greenhouses in the United States to be sold as houseplants.

The gloxinia is a member of the Gesneria plant family.

CAPE JASMINE GARDENIA
Scientific name: [*Gardenia jasminoides*]

Gardenias are large waxy white flowers that grow on shrubs. These flowers bloom naturally in tropical and subtropical regions. Gardenias are known for their wonderful fragrance.

These delicate flowers thrive at a temperature of about 60°F (15.6°C). They also need a moist environment. If the flower is exposed to cooler temperatures, its leaves turn yellow. Before long, the flower will wither.

In the United States, gardenias are raised in greenhouses. There the climate conditions necessary for these fragile flowers can be controlled. The Cape Jasmine gardenia is often admired for its impressive size and beauty. It is frequently a popular choice for corsages.

The white blossom is called the Cape Jasmine gardenia because it was originally brought to Europe from an English colony in Africa known as the Cape Colony. The gardenia is a member of the Rubiaceae plant family. Botanists placed it in this grouping because it grows on a treelike shrub.

Cape Jasmine Gardenia

African Violets

AFRICAN VIOLET
Scientific name: [*Saintpaulia ionantha*]

The African violet is a beautiful tropical plant that grows naturally in Africa. Its lovely flowers measure about an inch (2.5 cm) in diameter and develop in clusters of three or more blossoms. Each flower grows from a single slender stalk. There are many different cultivated varieties of African violets. Some have purple flowers; other plants bear pink or white blossoms.

African violets, which may grow to a height of about 5 inches (13 cm), have heart-shaped leaves, covered with fine hairs. African violets do best in soil that is rich in decaying matter.

Although African violets grow wild in the tropics, they are widely *cultivated* as houseplants in the United States. The attractive colorful flowers keep this plant in demand at many flower shops. Its scientific name honors the man who discovered this plant—Baron Walter von Saint Paul-Illaire. Despite its common name, the African violet is not a true violet. Instead, it's a member of the Gesneria plant family.

Bird-of-Paradise

BIRD-OF-PARADISE
Scientific name: [*Strelitzia reginae*]

The bird-of-paradise is a dazzling orange and blue three-petaled flower. These flowers rest in narrow, curved leaves. The flower is named after a group of magnificent birds that have been highly prized for their brilliantly colored plumage.

Although these flowers were originally discovered in South America, they can be found in other parts of the world too. In the United States, birds-of-paradise are now cultivated in warm areas such as Florida and California.

The bird-of-paradise is closely related to the banana family. This colorful exotic flower is lovely to look at. However, the bird-of-paradise can be as deadly as it is beautiful. Its seeds are poisonous if eaten.

GLOSSARY

arid—extremely dry; nearly barren from lack of water

botanist—a person trained in the science of plant life

chlorophyll—the green coloring matter of leaves and plants necessary for their production of food

cultivate—to develop or improve a plant through labor and care

greenhouse—a building made largely of glass in which plants are grown or protected

leaflet—division of compound leaf

medicinal—used to cure an illness or relieve pain

55

narcotic—a substance that soothes, calms, or makes drowsy

nectar—a sweet liquid given off by some flowers

species—a specific kind of plant or animal

thicket—a thick growth of small trees and shrubs

FOR FURTHER READING

Challand, Helen. *Plants without Seeds.* Chicago: Children's Press, 1986.

Cole, Joanna. *Plants in the Winter.* New York: Crowell, 1973.

Fichter, George S. *Wildflowers of North America.* New York: Random House, 1982.

Kirkpatrick, Rena K. *Look at Seeds and Weeds,* rev. ed. Milwaukee, Wisconsin: Raintree, 1985.

Panker, Philip. *Life Cycle of a Sunflower.* New York: Bookwright Press, 1988.

Podendorf, Illa. *Weeds and Wildflowers.* Chicago: Children's Press, 1981.

Pohl, Kathleen. *Morning Glories.* Milwaukee, Wisconsin: Raintree, 1986.

Sabin, Louis. *Plants, Seeds and Flowers.* Mahwah, New Jersey: Troll, 1985.

INDEX

ABOUT THE AUTHOR

Elaine Landau has been a newspaper reporter, a youth services librarian, and a children's book editor. She has written over twenty-five books for young people.

Ms. Landau lives in New Jersey, where she enjoys wild-flowers in the forests and fields and cultivates her own garden.